730.92 LAK

D0183021

Author: Janet Koplos
Editor: Matthew Koumis
Graphic Design: Rachael Dadd & MK
Reprographics: Ermanno Beverari
Printed in Italy by Grafiche AZ, Verona

© **Telos Art Publishing 2003**

Telos Limited
PO Box 125, Winchester
SO23 7UJ England
t: +44 (0) 1962 864546
f: +44 (0) 1962 864727
e: editorial@telos.net
e: sales@telos.net
w: www.telos.net

ISBN 1 902015 39 8 (softback)
ISBN 1 902015 55 6 (hardback)

A CIP catalogue record for this book
is available from The British Library

Photo Credits
Peter Macchia, John Friedman,
M Lee Fatherree, Debbie Stone,
Tom Grotta, Mat Laky, Jaques Gael
Cressaty, Marcia Wynes, Brett
Christiansen, Charlotte Seidl

Notes
All dimensions are shown in metric
and imperial, height x width x depth.

Publisher's Acknowledgements
Paul Richardson, John Denison, Sue
Atkinson, Erin Prues, Kristina
Detwiller, Freya, Simone, Ermanno.

illustration on page 1 and 48:
TiMe
2001
apple and plum prunings,
copper finish brads
22 x 22 x 1in (58 x 58 x 3cm)
Jill Butler Collection

The right of Gyöngy Laky, Janet Koplos
and James Melchert to be identified as
the authors of their work has been
asserted by them in accordance with
the Copyright, Designs and Patents
Act 1988. All rights reserved. No part
of this publication may be reproduced,
stored in a retrieval system or
transmitted in any form or by any
means, without the prior permission
in writing of the publishers.
Photocopying this book is illegal.

portfolio collection
Gyöngy Laky

TELOS

Affirmative No. 1 1996
plied and sewn telephone wire
8 x 8 x 8in (21 x 21 x 21cm)
Robert and Judy Aptekar Collection
BrownGrotta Gallery, Connecticut

BARTON PEVERIL
COLLEGE LIBRARY
EASTLEIGH SO50 5ZA

Contents

Foreword by James Melchert

Gyöngy Laky draws inspiration easily from multiple sources and traditions with seemingly insatiable curiosity that has rewarded her with a full quiver of forms and ideas to investigate. The formats she chooses run from the intimacy of hand scale to large outdoor installations, and from freestanding letters and words to lacy abstractions across a wall or hillside. Conceptually, her work references the ingenuity inherent in how human beings structure and restructure their environments. She is a master at juxtaposing materials drawn from both natural and industrial processes and at making dissonance work for her.

Laky's love of architecture and of how things are put together is evident throughout her oeuvre. While there are echoes in her work of influences at the University of California, Berkeley, where she studied with both Ed Rossbach and Peter Voulkos, the principle sources that inform her projects are in the openwork patterns of bridges, scaffolding, or the skeletal grids of high-rise buildings.

For all the density of her massive constructions, the entwining elements that form them have a character and elegance of their own. Even the simplest of her compositions, which read much like flat drawings, have an inner pulse that animate them.

The visual surprises and pleasures that Laky gives us with her work have understandably won her a wide audience. Laky has helped bring new life to fiber art by stretching the boundaries of how we define it. It isn't just the objects that she places in the landscape that are new, it is the landscape itself that her work has helped change.

James Melchert
Professor Emeritus of Art,
University of California, Berkeley
Former Director of Visual Arts Program,
National Endowment of the Arts

Gyöngy Laky: Connections
by Janet Koplos

In The Crowd
1999
finished pine,
vinyl-coated steel nails
11 x 24 x 24in
(29 x 63 x 63cm)

Gyöngy Laky's artistic production over a 30-year career can be divided into three quite different categories. She has made large-scale installations, both indoors and out. Her language-based sculptures, relatively few in number, are probably her most widely known works. Most numerous by far are the baskets. The clarity and force with which the works embody her intellectual concerns link these disparate groups. That they are visually appealing as well seems almost an accident, or at least the product of instinct rather than deliberation: Laky is not seeking to charm or to please, but to explore or to deeply engage.

Her art is not in any obvious way autobiographical or expressionistic. Yet even art that seems impersonal does not emerge out of thin air; Laky's mindset and the particular things that appeal to her are inextricably bound to aspects of her life and experience.

Laky was born in Hungary in 1944 (her name is pronounced approximately *Jinj Locky*). Her family fled their homeland when she was a child and eventually settled in Carmel, California, where her father ran a gallery of modern art and her mother was a painter. Laky was a student at the University of California, Berkeley, in the mid-60s. That was a time not only of student rebellions, the Free Speech Movement, the birth of the environmental movement, cooperatives and natural foods, but also of the extraordinary design department that proved so influential to the contemporary craft field. While at Berkeley, Laky studied with Ed Rossbach who had an appreciable influence on her as is discussed later. Meanwhile, her brother and most of her friends were in architecture, and she developed a deep interest in aboriginal and vernacular architecture. In 1971, she spent a year in India.

Combine these factors and you could not fail to get something interesting. Since her college days, Laky has been an activist. She returned from India and started an unconventional textile school – *Fiberworks* – 1973. She has stayed true to the ideal with which she started Fiberworks, that of inviting people to give workshops in whatever subjects interested them. It originally consisted of creative, accomplished people giving workshops in whatever subjects interested them. In an 80s 'open studio' event, she demonstrated what she called 'textile thinking', a term that in itself conveys her characteristic attitude.

Also in the 80s, she participated in the founding of the environmental design department and more recently the development of a master of fine arts program at the University of California, Davis, where she teaches. She was chair of the art department for two years in the 90s and has been a proponent of affirmative action for women and others at the university. This brief history shows that she has not proceeded in a narrow, straight line, nor by way of predictable steps. Neither has her art.

This brief history shows that she has not proceeded in a narrow, straight line, nor by way of predictable steps.
Neither has her art.

Installations

The installations that Laky began to make in the early 1980s have taken a dazzling variety of forms. An early example is the *Yellow, Blue and Red pieces* of 1984, in which she used surveyors' tape to make grids or fabric-like meshes in the California landscape. In *Yellow Piece*, for example, she ran the golden tape over a 100 by 125 foot (30 x 38 meter) expanse of hillside. The grid format, which in the 60s and 70s had come to prominence in the art world in both two-dimensional and three-dimensional works, was not a novelty in fiber, since it is intrinsic to the creation of many woven textiles and much basketry. The textile grid tends to show spontaneous, imprecise relationships involving subtle variations, rather than rigid perfection.

Laky's innovation was to use the grid on a scale that dwarfed the usual ambitions of fiber – a scale that was seen in contemporary fiber only in the revived Lausanne Biennial of Tapestry. She creatively expanded upon a use of fiber extrinsic to the fiberart field: in these landscape works, she cleverly found a natural outdoor use of fiber and applied it in the manner of sculpture and textiles. Happily, she was able to use color – an important aspect of her work despite not employing the chromatic variety and intensity that yarns can offer.

She created a three-dimensional work that emphasized surface rather than mass. Both the grid organization and the surveyor's material itself have been used to regularize nature, and thus call to mind the contrary aspects of the American relationship to the land – civilizing on one hand, despoiling on the other. These grid pieces can not be called 'typical'; there is no typical form or material in Laky's installations.

Falling Up
1985
painted wood slats, string
site-specific installation:
Musée des Arts Décoratifs,
Louvre, Paris

'Falling Up', 1985, consisted of suspended bars of painted wood that suggested both motion and form as they drew the eye to the ceiling and beyond, to infinity. It was surprising how different the work looked from various viewpoints. From the side it seemed to be a freeze-frame picture of the levitation of sticks, but from above it loosely defined a container shape, a circular form closing at the bottom – that is, a basket.

Also in the 80s she suspended color-wrapped twigs to make drawings in space, and plaited paper rope to make both confining and expanding forms. *Falling Up* (1985), consisted of suspended bars of painted wood that suggested both motion and form as they drew the eye to the ceiling and beyond, to infinity. Despite the fact that the elements were uninflected, there was a surprising degree of implied movement. Also surprising was how different the work looked from various viewpoints. From the side it seemed to be a freeze-frame picture of the levitation of sticks, but from above it loosely defined a container shape, a circular form closing at the bottom – that is, a basket. Perhaps, with this contrast, Laky meant the work to suggest the value of different perspectives.

In 1991, in England, she made a large willow cylinder, which, seen on end, framed a landscape view. But from the side, the cylinder was an obstruction, both physically and visually.

The obstruction theme continued in a 1993 indoor installation (made in collaboration with students) consisted of an openwork enclosure that was essentially transparent yet controlled the viewer's passage through space. In 1998, she surrounded a tree with a 5 foot (1.5 meter) stack of split firewood that made a vision-blocking, brick-like wall and offered only limited physical access to the tree. In this variety, we see Laky's determined curiosity and plucky exploration.

Drawing with the Desert Wind
Laky in Panamint Valley,
California, 1983

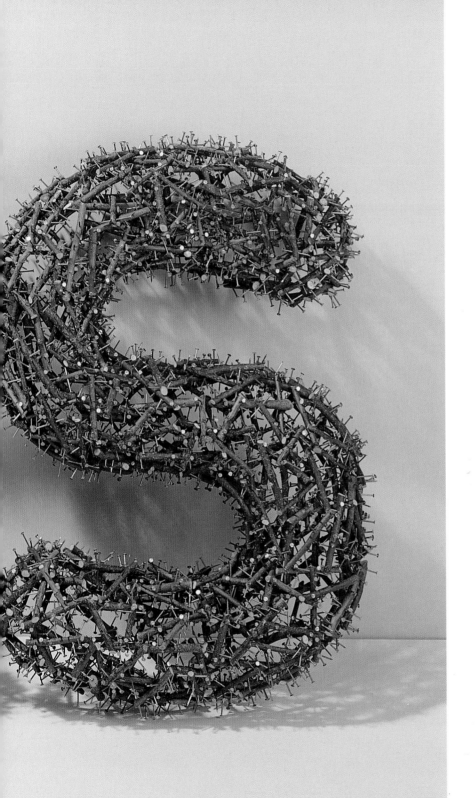

Word Works

A wide range can also be seen in Laky's use of language in her art over the last 15 years. She has treated words as freestanding structures, as precious objects and as contained gestures. She uses words that are powerful in their declarative simplicity – such as 'YES' and 'NO' – and which resonate with meaning.

In what may be her single best-known work, 90 inch (2.2 meter) tall letters made of pruned tree limbs bundled over a steel armature spell out the word 'ART'. Each letter is multiplied: an 'A' repeated twice more constructs a pyramid, four joined 'R' forms are square in plan, while the letter 'T' in three incarnations has a triangular configuration. Each is a symbol and a structure.

Negative
1998
apple prunings doweled with
vinyl-coated steel nails
29 x 60 x 8in (76 x 156 x 21cm)
Private collection, Colorado

"It becomes something more when one learns that the title is 'That Word.' The title might be read with a sigh or a shudder, and it calls to mind the ambivalent status of the fiber field and the mixed attitudes of its practitioners, who want recognition in the larger art world but are not willing to give up the values of textiles to obtain it...".

That Word
1989
orchard prunings and electrical wire
on welded substructure
each letter: 90 x 54 x 54in
(234 x 141 x 141cm)

This 1989 work, which was exhibited at the 14th Lausanne Biennale, has impressive scale and graphic impact, to say the least. But it becomes something more when one learns that the title is *That Word*. The title might be read with a sigh or a shudder. It calls to mind the ambivalent status of the fiber field and the mixed attitudes of its practitioners, who want recognition in the larger art world but are not willing to give up the values of textiles to obtain it. That word, 'art', is used in the field as a plea, an epithet or a cudgel, and it looms large: Laky manages to allude to all of this in her sculpture.

Other word works are freestanding, though none adopt the same degree of complex three-dimensionality as *That Word*. Laky has, however, repeatedly devised layered meanings. Another significant word work is *Protest: Naught for Naught*, which she created for an Austrian exhibition called *Art in the Landscape V* in 2000.

The letters 'N' and 'O' are again formed of prunings, in this case enmeshed to suggest basketry style, rather than bundled. The small 'N' lies on the ground, as if shoved over; the much larger 'O', 10 feet (3 meters) tall, is both an exclamation and a frame isolating a little piece of the world. The title and the venue point to a political statement: the ascendancy of a right-wing political party in Austria had led to protests by citizens and boycotts from abroad. Laky opted to participate in the exhibition with a complex piece in which basketry can be read as a plea for transparency or as alluding to the entanglements of central Europe's modern history. The 'O' is also the form of a zero. Combine this with the 'Naught' in the title, the informal use of 'aught' to mean 'nothing' and the homonymic 'ought' suggesting moral necessity.

Wake
2000
apple and pear prunings, nails
50 x 50 x 2in
(130 x 130 x 6cm)

The small 'N' lies on the ground, as if shoved over; the much larger 'O',
10 feet tall, is both an exclamation and a frame isolating a little piece of the world.

Art in the Landscape V 2000
Installation for 'Kunst in der Landschaft V,' Austria
Protest: Naught for Naught
orchard prunings, screws
48 x 48 x 16in (125 x 125 x 42cm) [N],
120 x 120 x 36in (312 x 312 x 94cm) [O]

The title and the venue point to a political statement: the ascendancy of a right-wing political party in Austria had led to protests by citizens and boycotts from abroad.

Of Course
apple prunings, vinyl-coated
steel nails
55 x 55 x 2in (143 x 143 x 6cm)

Most of her other word works, however, are playful, including earlier uses of the word "NO" such as *Affirmative No. 1* (1996), in which the cheerful colors of telephone wire are as agreeable as the open-and-closed, transparent-and-dense balance of the two letters. The 'N' is a grid construction and the 'O' more like tapestry or felt. Likewise, her making of the word 'WIRE' from its subject material (1994) and her use of prunings to form the word 'TWIG' on the wall (1998) are amusing rather than confrontational.

Laky has no declared position on why she is attracted to words as a subject matter, though she considers the possibility that her multilingual experience as an immigrant child may have made her particularly sensitive to the nature of language. Her approach nearly seems like concrete poetry: the words are given substance, weight, depth, position.

Their palpability draws them out in thought, just as Samuel Beckett's character relishes the sensation of the word 'spool' in his mouth and ear in *Krapp's Last Tape*. Laky is notably articulate – her own best spokesman for her ideas – and as a sculptor she has been able to realize her language tangibly.

At the same time, she has made several word works that dissolve to line or to negative shape (emptiness). *Of Course* (1998) consists of a wavy grid made of apple prunings, subdivided into nine blocks, each in turn consisting of nine smaller squares. At the center of each block is an individualistic line. One might guess that the diagonal line in the top left block represents N, and that the inverted V in the top center indicates an A, and so on, until finally this modern cuneiform spells out 'naturally', equivalent to the title.

Line (1992), is a word picture. Neat capital letters spell the title. In the middle of the first and last letters are simple representations of open eyes. This cheeky artwork returns the viewer's gaze. Laky seems to see the grid as a flexible structure, a system of spaces that can be filled with any other system of communicative markings – language or image – in a cross-genre synergy.

In her word works Laky uses mostly capital letters, which are straighter and more visually emphatic than lower-case letters. Thus letterforms are linked to the rest of her work by her predilection for straight or nearly straight lines throughout her oeuvre. The landscape grids, the suspended drawings, the willow cylinder all rely on straight lines, each in its own way.

Baskets

Laky's characteristic baskets are also unusually rectilinear for their genre: most are bristly and irregular. Only in her earliest works did she regularly plait, weave, twine or use any other technique of fine basketry. Instead she has made a practice of simply gathering together somewhat stiff materials and fixing them in overlapping relationships sufficient to suggest a container form. The walls often make one think of screens; the view into or through the basket makes a sharper impression than its silhouette. Viewers may respond to the assertive individual elements as strongly as to the whole.

Laky's favored basketry material is the prunings that she obtains from public and private sources such as park or street trees and orchards.

Twigs are less common in basketry than reeds, vines or bamboo, but they serve Laky's environmental interests, since she is recycling what is essentially waste. Also prunings are available free, which appeals to her pragmatism.

To these materials she adds unusual complements, such as screws and telephone wire. Unconventional materials perhaps came with her training at Berkeley, under Rossbach, who was known for the experimentation in his own work as well as that which he encouraged in his students. Laky's early use of plastics may owe something to Rossbach, something to the ethic of reuse that impressed her in India, and something to basic frugality.

Stain
2000
toothpicks, paint
6in high x 16in diameter
(16 x 42cm)
Nancy Margolis Gallery, New York

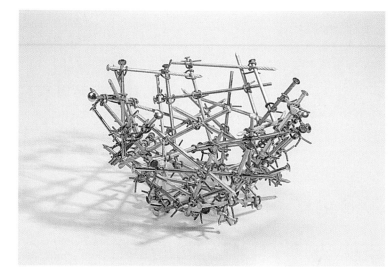

Fish Storm 1982
cardboard, plastic, staples
24in diameter (65cm)
Charles A. Wustum Museum of Fine Arts,
Racine, Wisconsin

Industrial Prunings
1993
aluminum nails, electrical wire
8in high x 13in diameter (21 x 34cm)
'Tools as Art,' The Hechinger Collection

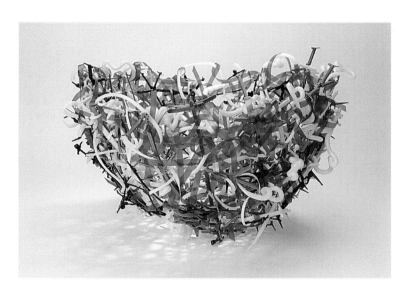

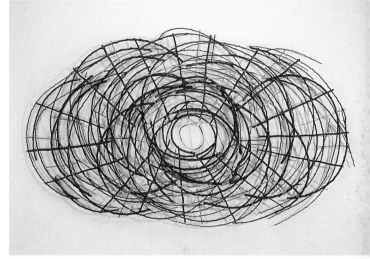

Graceful Exit
1994
plastic remainders from Johnson Wax Co.
13in high x 21in diameter (34 x 55cm)
Adele and Gene Hoffman Collection

Sun Stream
1994
apricot prunings, wire, plastic
48 x 72 x 4in (125 x 188 x 11cm)
Barry and Irene Fisher Collection

Pacific Lace

2001

telephone wire

3in high x 7in diam. (8 x 19cm)

Irene and Barry Fisher Collection

In the 70s she made baskets of filmy plastic vegetable bags, while *Graceful Exit* (1995) is made of discards from the Johnson's Wax factory: blue, red, white, yellow and purple pieces of plastic, tangled together.

Her early experiments had to do with investigating form as much as with exploring materials. This, too, may be the legacy of Rossbach, who she thinks of as "making a print on fabric one day and a plaited-newspaper basket the next." There is "something about working with flexible materials that encourages flexibility and movement in thinking," she asserts. Her works have included nets, stuffed tubes and some rather predatory – looking objects – as much spider or trap as basket. Some flat, mesh-like works were made of paper, cloth, random fibers and whatnot. She stiffened ropes with glue so that they would stand up on their own like charmed snakes.

A very few of her basketry pieces have involved closed surfaces. One such is *Fish Storm* (1982) made of cardboard strips and plastic, stapled. A blue, yellow or black border around each piece of cardboard gives this elegantly full form a bright punch.

She has made more open experiments in a variety of materials, such as wire mesh skewered together with nails in *After Charcoal* (1985). *Sun Stream* (1995) is a flat wall piece measuring 48 by 72 by 4 inches (122 x1 83 x 10cm). It looks as if an open basket of apricot prunings and a few bits of colored wire had been pressed by a steamroller into a gracefully looping sunburst.

It's interesting to note that Laky's . unorthodox materials have tended to be used as connective devices rather than being the structural substance of the basket, in the Rossbach manner.

Laky's favored basketry material is the prunings that she obtains from public and private sources such as park or street trees and orchards. Twigs are less common in basketry than reeds, vines or bamboo, but they serve Laky's environmental interests, since she is recycling what is essentially waste. Prunings also are available free, which appeals to her pragmatism.

Spike 1998
apple prunings, vinyl coated steel nails
13in high x 21in diameter (34 x 55cm)
Smithsonian Institution National
Museum of American Art, Renwick Gallery

above:

Noise at Noon 1996
apple prunings, cable ties
24in high (63cm)
Ann Hatch Collection

left:

Old Names 1994
brass drawer labels, telephone wire
8in high x 25in diameter (21 x 65cm)
Private collection, Florida

Telephone wire holds together the plum prunings of *Small World* (1999). In this piece, single colors of wire spiral down the lengths of robust-looking, diagonally interwoven twigs, creating lively zigzags of bright color amid the soberness of the twigs' brown bark. In the same year, Laky assembled slender pieces of milled pine, in short lengths that she spiked together with vinyl-coated steel nails and titled *In the Crowd*. In a 24-inch (61cm) diameter bowl, the rigidity of the lumber contrasts with its light hue – which seems buoyant – and the transparency of its sparse structure. The nails, little browned slivers, give the whole an inflated, prickly quality.

Desert Edge (2001) has a similar light color, but its round eucalyptus branches, which have a softer, almost corky appearance, are held together with deck screws, an even more aggressive method of joining.

In *Noise at Noon* (1996) regular lengths of straight, thin apple prunings are stacked horizontally in a sort of log-cabin arrangement but without orderly corners, bright blue cable ties fastening them. The short, glossy, water-hue lines of the ties create an impression of stylized rain or water trickling down a pile of logs.

Laky has also constructed baskets entirely of telephone wire, as in the colorful mesh of *Pacific Lace* (2001), and entirely of toothpicks, in the red-streaked low bowl called *Stain* (2000). Another unusual material is brass drawer labels: in *Old Names* (1994) she lashed together these small rectangles using telephone wire. Arranging them both vertically and horizontally, sometimes partly overlapped and sometimes abutted, she was able to make a gracefully rounded basket lattice.

Laky's innovation was to use the grid on a scale that dwarfed the usual ambitions of fiber – a scale that was seen in contemporary fiber only in the revived Lausanne Biennial of Tapestry.

Yellow Piece 1984
Landmarks Exhibition: W. Wiley and G. Laky
Headlands Center for the Arts,
Sausalito, California
125 x 100ft (390 x 312m) one of three parts

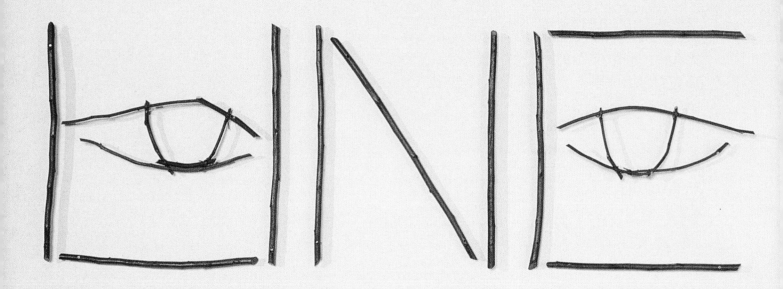

That same year she defined a solid basket shape with wine corks laid end to end in horizontal rows, nailing them together almost invisibly. Exceptionally, for *Industrial Prunings* (1993) she used a connective element as her constructive material by wiring aluminum nails together in a shape easily recalling a basket, but considerably less friendly in character.

'Industrial prunings' is a term she has frequently used, paired with 'orchard prunings'. It's a clever way of expressing availability and selection from the modern world, without restriction. It illustrates again her feeling for words. Laky has a gift for seemingly simple and clear titles that never diminish the works.

In these titles, as in the permutations of basketry forms and materials that she has explored over the years, one can almost see her brain working. She turns things around. She considers what an irreducible essence would be.

What makes a basket? For Laky, a basket seems to boil down to connected lines suggesting a volume – as broad a definition as that. So she can play with materials, with construction, with particularities of shape, indulging her experimental urge within a comfortable, knowable format, the basket with its wealth of pleasant human associations. She can make this age-old invention specific to our times by blending apparently unrelated materials, this blend then symbolizing the exciting juxtapositions•of a global culture.

Her combinations often allude to the architectonic nature of baskets. They make one think of how the building of a house can relate to the building of a basket. Laky tugs basketry techniques in the direction of carpentry – applied architecture rather than theory. Her works emphasize labor as distinct, discrete steps, not the fluid interlacing so common to basketry or the free gestures of painting or glazing.

Line 1992
plum and acacia prunings
11 x 36 x 1in (29 x 94 x 3cm)
Nancy Jewel Collection

Process is visible and labor-intense, recalling the "basic forms of human ingenuity" that have always impressed her.

In the final analysis, Laky's work is distinguished by its connections, in two senses of the word. One is the connection she draws between seemingly disparate things and ideas, such as industry and nature, the current and the age-old. The other is the literal connection that is so frequently emphasized in her works, through enlarged or unexpected linking devices, from screws to plastic ties to the hand-carved and hand-painted dowels that pinion twigs in many of her works.

These physical connections are so prominent, and so consistent in their emphasis, that one must ask why, and what they mean. Laky's personal history of connection between the Old World and the New seems to be an appropriate analogy, and her counterculture collaborations are another instance of meaningful connections.

Other artists, such as John Garrett, have devoted themselves to non-natural basketry materials. Other artists, such as Dorothy Gill Barnes, have used robust wooden elements rather than those that can be bent. Other artists, such as John McQueen, have used plastic ties for their convenience and irreverence. And of course many artists have made land art, installations, and artworks incorporating language. But Laky's inquisitive bent has enabled her, and encouraged her, to reach across forms and genres, and it is the connections in her art – writ large and writ small – that make it as engaging, exciting, provoking and beautiful as it is.

Janet Koplos
Senior Editor, *Art in America*

Valley House 1998
plum prunings with drywall bullets
19 x 24 x 16in (50 x 63 x 42cm)
Jonathan Cohen Collection

Biography

Born

1944   Budapest, Hungary

Education

1970 - 71   BA & MA University of California, Berkeley

1971 - 72   UC Professional Studies in India Program

Public Collections

Sacramento Metropolitan Arts Commission, Art in Public Places Program, Sacramento City
Council Chambers, Sacramento, California

Federal Government Art-in-Architecture Program, Social Security
Administration Building, Richmond, California

Contemporary Art Society of London

LongHouse Reserve, East Hampton, New York

The Charles A. Wustum Museum of Fine Arts, Racine, Wisconsin

Renwick Gallery, National Museum of American Art, Smithsonian Institution, Washington DC

Philadelphia Museum of Art, Philadelphia

The Arkansas Arts Center, Little Rock, Arkansas

American Craft Museum, New York

Monterey Peninsula Museum of Art, Monterey, California

Oakland Museum, Oakland, California

San Francisco Museum of Modern Art, San Francisco, California

Savaria Museum, Szombathely, Hungary

The Contemporary Museum, Honolulu

Professional Participation

2000 - 02	Founding Board Member, National Basketry Organization.
1988 - 92	Trustee, American Crafts Council
	(Chair, Board of Overseers, Information Center)
1986 - 1992	Member, Board of Directors, Capp Street Project, San Francisco
	(Chair 1986 - 89)
1978 - present	Professor, University of California, Davis, CA
	(Chair, Department of Art, 1995-1997)
1973 - 77	Founder and Executive Director, Fiberworks,
	Center for the Textile Arts, Berkeley

Selected Solo Exhibitions

2001	Nancy Margolis Gallery, New York
	MX Gallery, Barcelona
1999	Officinet Gallery, Danske Kunsthåndværkere, Copenhagen
	Memorial Union Gallery, University of California, Davis
1996	Royal Institute of British Architects Gallery, Manchester, UK
1985	Site 311 Gallery, Pacific Grove, California
1984	Monterey Peninsula Museum of Art, California
1982	Meyer, Breier, Weiss, San Francisco
	Pence Gallery, Davis

Selected Two-person Exhibitions

1996 and 93	Brown Grotta Gallery, Wilton Connecticut.
1986	Wita Gardiner Gallery, San Diego, California.
1981	Sarospatak Museum, Sarospatak, Hungary.

Selected Group Exhibitions

2002	'The Renwick Invitational' (Koehler, Laky, Logan and Rawdin)
	National Museum of American Art, Smithsonian Institution, Washington DC,
	'2nd International Tapestry Art: from Lausanne to Beijing,'
	Academy of Arts and Design, Tsinghua University, Beijing, China
	'5ème Festival International de la Tapisserie et d l'Art de la Fibre,' Beauvais, France
	'Small Works in Fiber,' LongHouse Reserve, East Hampton, New York, (international tour))
	'Baskets Now: USA,' Arkansas Art Center, Little Rock
2001	'Crossover,' Bury St Edmunds Art Gallery, England (tour)
2000	'Made in California 1900-2000,' Los Angeles County Museum, Los Angeles
	'Nature Re-Bound,' Palo Alto Art Center, Palo Alto, California
	'Kunst in der Landschaft V,' Prigglitz, Austria
	'In Focus,' Sotheby's, London
1999	'Material Witness: Masters of California Crafts,' Crocker Art Museum, Sacramento, CA
	'Contemporary International Basketmaking,' Crafts Council of Britain and
	The Whitworth Art Gallery, University of Manchester, England, (tour)
1998	'Ting '98,' Konsthantverks, Kulturföreningen KLAR, Ransäter, Sweden
	'Threads, Contemporary American Basketry' (*Inventing America:*
	A year of American Culture) Barbican Centre, London

Selected Group Exhibitions continued

1998	'98 Miniartextil Como: Ottava Rassegna, Internazionale d'Arte Tessile'
	Innocenzo XI, ex Area Ticosa in Viale, Como, Italy
1995	'Art in Nature,' Sun Valley Center for the Arts and Humanities, Sun Valley, ID
1991	'Eventails,' Galerie Philharmonie, Liege, Belgium (tour: Spain, France,
	Netherlands, Hungary, Yugoslavia)
1990	'Fibers: United States/Colombia,' Florida State University,
	Tallahassee, FL/Universidad de Los Andes, Colombia,
1989	'14e Biennale Internationale de la Tapisserie,'
	Musée Cantonal des Beaux Arts, Lausanne, Switzerland
	(tour: Nederlands Textielmuseum, Tlburg, The Netherlands)

Selected Events, Art Actions, Site-specific and Situational Works

1998	*Tree House,* site-specific work for the exhibition: 'Complex Harbor,'
	Art Complex Museum, Wustum, Massachusetts
1993	*Surroundings,* Art Gallery, California State University, Chico, site-specific installation.
1991	*Sounding Form,* site-specific work,'New Forms in Willow,' Projects Environment,
	Ness Gardens, University of Liverpool, England
1989	*Forms for Language*, site-specific work, 'Landscape and Sculpture,' Projects Environment,
	Manchester Metropolitan University, England
1987	*Improvisational Structures: Line, Movement, Change and Space*, site-specific work,
	Concordia University, Montreal, Quebec, Canada
1985	*Falling Up,* Musée des Arts Decoratifs, site-specific work in conjunction
	with the exhibition 'Fibres-Art 85,' Paris, France

Selected Publications

2000	Dugdale, Juanita. 'Gyöngy Laky – matter and message,'
	Baseline International Graphics, no 32, Bradbourne Publishers Ltd, UK
2000	Lonning, Kari. *The Art of Basketry*, Sterling Publishing Co. New York
2000	Leier, Ray; Peters, Jan; Wallace, Kevin. *Baskets, Tradition & Beyond*,
	Guild Publishing, Madison, WI
1999	Butcher, Mary. *Contemporary International Basketmaking*,
	Merrell Holberton, London, England
1998	Edwards, Irene; Eccles, Graham. *Video: Ten American Makers,* Odyssey, USA
1985	Thomas, Michael; Mainguy, Christine; Pommier, Sophie. *Textile Art*,
	Skira/Rizzoli, Geneva, Switzerland; New York, NY (French and English version)

Desert Edge 2001
eucalyptus prunings with deck screws
9in high x 19in diameter (24 x 50cm)
The Contemporary Museum, Honolulu

BARTON PEVERIL
COLLEGE LIBRARY
EASTLEIGH SO50 5ZA